dick bruna

my vest
is white

Tate Publishing

my vest is white

my socks are
red

my shirt is yellow

my dress is red

my ribbons
are yellow

my shoes are black

yellow

red

black

my coat is
blue

my scarf is
yellow

my hat is green

my gloves are red

green

yellow

blue

red

black

Other Dick Bruna books available from Tate Publishing:

I can count 2012
round, square, triangle 2012
miffy the artist 2008

Published 2012 by order of the Tate Trustees
by Tate Publishing, a division of Tate Enterprises Ltd,
Millbank, London SW1P 4RG
www.tate.org.uk/publishing

Original edition: *mijn hemd is wit*
Original text Dick Bruna © copyright Mercis Publishing bv, 1972
Illustrations Dick Bruna © copyright Mercis bv, 1972
Publication licensed by Mercis Publishing bv, Amsterdam
Printed by Sachsendruck Plauen GmbH, Germany
All rights reserved.

A catalogue record for this book is available from the British Library
ISBN 978 1 84976 075 1
Distributed in the United States and Canada by ABRAMS, New York
Library of Congress Control Number: applied for